Yes and No

Books by John Skoyles

Poetry

A Little Faith
Permanent Change
Definition of the Soul
The Situation
Suddenly It's Evening: Selected Poems
Inside Job

Prose

Generous Strangers
Secret Frequencies: A New York Education
A Moveable Famine: A Life in Poetry
The Nut File
Driven

Yes and No

John Skoyles

Carnegie Mellon University Press
Pittsburgh 2021

Acknowledgments

My thanks to the editors of the journals in which the following poems first appeared:

The Atlantic: "The Heart Has Reasons"
Barrow Street: "The River Twice"
Copper Nickel: "The Letters"
Ibbetson Street: "Oncle Lily" and "Love Poem (Tentative Title)"
On the Seawall: "Blame," "Prayer at the Masked Ball," and "Unwritten"
The New Yorker: "My Mother, Heidegger and Derrida"
The Paris Review: "The Second Olga"
Plume: "Alphabet," "Friends in Dreams," "It," "Last Words, Last Rites, Last Acts,"
    "The Blue Sea Motel," and "The Revenants"
Plume 6: New Poems 2017: "Here and There"
Plume Poetry 9: "Kitten Cat Kitten"
Poetry: "Self-Help"
SALT: "That's the Hell We're In"
The Yale Review: "His Shirt"

Alcatraz: Anthology of Prose/Poetry: "The Death of Zero"

Cover art: Varujan Boghosian, *The Minister's Black Veil*, 2009, 14 1/2 x 12 1/2
Private Collection, through the courtesy of Berta Walker Gallery, Provincetown.

Designed by Trevor Lazar

Library of Congress Control Number 2021937533
ISBN 978-0-88748-673-9
Copyright © 2021 by John Skoyles

10 9 8 7 6 5 4 3 2 1

for Anne Turner Beletic

Goodbye to the Life I used to Live—
And the world I used to Know—

                    —*Emily Dickinson*

Contents

I

Friends in Dreams

The pond flattered the foliage,
and our reflections

trembled at the rim,
as if showing

we were souls
in skin that would fall

from us like these leaves
this autumn.

We no longer breathed
between sand and sky—

we were with friends in dreams.
A kiss disappeared

in the mist near her face,
my palm passed

through his outstretched hand.
One turned the tarot deck,

another walked on his knees
down the center aisle

of the Church of the Typical Inhabitant
and at the rail

lit the wick of a burned-down vow.
I was enjoying my role

in this eternal animation
among friends in dreams,

when the best of them,
pierced by a diagnosis,

called from an office
outside my reverie

with the news
and the need

to leave the world
of make-believe,

asking that I take him home.
And there he was,

at the waiting room
window,

staring into the sheer
sunlit maze

of streets and avenues
that ended here.

Love and Death

How easily the fallen autumn leaves
become letters I write to you,

describing how they stall
then vault across the road,

and how quickly
common things spark

a roll call of those who
have entered that gated district

called the underworld,
where devils and saints

trade roles in retold tales
involving keepsakes.

In my case, relics placed
along the bookshelf—

a signet ring, cigarette lighter,
and the Holy Ghost medal

my mother wore to recover
her lost voice.

I take each trinket in hand
and stand before a thousand volumes

that address just two issues:
love and death.

Are there any other stories
beyond these simple plots?

Yes—are we connected
to the infinite, or not?

My mother's voice returned
when the spirit leapt

from that cold medallion's
tongue of flame

she locked around her neck.
The carnelian's carved elaborate S

my father purchased
during World War II

while his shipmates spent
their shore leave pay

on alcohol and tattoos.
He swore the stone grew warm

at shifts in weather,
luck or love.

My uncle spun a path
across Fifth Avenue at dusk,

flicking this lighter
with his thumb as if seized by a set

of strings from above,
while I, the boy beside him,

held out my palms
to apologize and halt traffic

at the same time.
What caused my mother's silence?

The fire in my uncle's brain?
Was that ring more than just for show?

Will a book on this shelf
tell their stories? Yes and no.

The Revenants

Meet the late Maurice Ravel,
his bolero banned and his name

damned as a bar to heaven
and a door to hell

at the Convent of the Seven Sorrows.
Enter my colleague

in critical theory
who analyzed the horizon

from the bottom
of a well,

and tried to understand
the tides by kicking

over a bucket of brine.
I bring your attention to

the Baroness von Tyebell-Schmidlein,
whose burning passions

cremated time
until her life was ash.

Here's Preston, her son,
fresh from his yoga mat,

who inhaled god everywhere,
like air, but shot himself

on mother's day,
her white gloves in his lap.

Why this parade of revenants
down the page?

I've tried my best to prevent
the last breath

of my friend on his deathbed
by introducing this circus

of the marvelous and strange,
and it worked.

I mean, it gave him
a final smile.

With a quick turn
of his head, he said,

"Why look so sad,
when you've brought

Ravel and the Baroness
back from the dead?"

The River Twice

Although they say you can't
cross the same river twice,

you can get caught
remembering that river,

its sodden bank
and charging water,

the place you brought
your daughter, son

and eager Labrador,
swam with Gus,

the grave digger,
and Doug, a father

of conceptual art.
It was a world apart,

and although they say you can't
turn back the clock,

you can get caught
remembering your father

taking you to the shore
with a flashlight

in the middle of the night
and returning wave-worn

with a pail of eels,
having traded

the blinding dark
for the blinding dawn.

Two Lives

The old dog's lost
his hearing,

something in common
with his master,

along with no longer
wearing a collar.

But there's a good deal
of dignity

in his static reply
to the beach crowd

pressing him to fetch
a frisbee from the sea.

This urgent request
to retrieve the past

invites an undertow
of grief from both sides

of the exchange.
At bedtime,

I notice the dog has given up
circling his mat

and just collapses.
A breeze through

the open window excites,
only slightly,

the sleeping canine's
olfactory sense,

and that same draft
approaches my desk

without permission
or consent,

slowly turning
the pages of a book

one by one,
and then quickly,

many at a time,
as if in a hurry

to get to the end.

Hamden

One lukewarm winter
I found myself
in the mirror of a condo

in Hamden,
the kind of place
where one either starts out

or ends up,
among chairs like those
in airports:

taut cushions
and steel tubing,
but rising from them here

takes you nowhere
except to a full-length mirror
where I lost myself

against a backdrop
of no snow
and a confining virus,

my reflection caught
in a mirror
itself caught in a frame

I walked toward
but not from,
always approaching

but never leaving
that stunted hallway
in Hamden,

a man, admit it,
at the tail-end of virility,
pulse no longer

the rising drumbeat
urging an addition
to the census,

but a polite nod
to the fertility gods,
a name taped to a mailbox,

a two-dimensional
apparition of the freight
of a former self

and its multifaceted
fractured past
pressed flat

against a glass veneer—
squatter, tenant,
survivor of certain

flu-like purges,
hoping for eviction
and fearful of it.

Joanne and Anne

I'm taking dictation
from the sounds and syllables

coming through the walls
of this downtown row house.

Anne on the left, Joanne
on the right,

and no Anne here in bed
where I am

an audience of one.
I haven't heard the word

zirconia in years,
but it has just appeared

on this page,
courtesy of Joanne's TV

bombarding my headboard.
After the tall tales of night

comes the wide truth of morning
and, with it, the broadcast news—

sirens, an interview
with the bereaved

and a reporter's claim
that others of our kind

will never be the same.
Anne and Joanne

are soon on the phone,
and I'm slowly being brought to life

by the force of an invisible
humanity around me,

a clerk to their overheard
emphatic words:

plosives without lips,
gutturals without throats.

Yet silence is worse,
like the diminished voice

in my journals and notes
recording the lullaby shuffle

of playing cards
and cascading plastic chips

that accompanied
my infant sleep

in the poker-mad
house where I was born.

Anne and Joanne,
Joanne and Anne—

cultivators of rooftop shrubbery,
suppliers of seed

to chickadees,
Argus-eyed behind venetian blinds—

once alive to more than these
before fate stung them

with the art of surviving.
They lean coupons and recipes

against each other's
double-locked doors

before they slide inside
and open their arms

to the world
beyond their walls,

and they and I begin to fly.

Self-Help

I was someone in the distance
who never got closer.

I lived in the past, so the present
was my future.

When I shook hands, I dissolved
into a mirror

where I tended
my reflection

of features so faint
my mother

strained to see them.
I was the rind, the zest,

a heart marooned
in the guest of a friend

in the back row
of a twelve-step room.

I confessed to the priest
in his box, suppressed

the north, south, east and west
desires that pull men

over the moon.
I crooned the self-help

tune that every glance
was a gift, every second

chance a first,
the suicide fence

on the tall bridge
a positive thing

for those crawling the walls.

One

The only one
is the one

you lost
and the one

you found,
so the only

one
is two,

though at first
light

it seems
that beneath

each
is something else,

a tree
or a leaf,

a giant
or an elf.

The only one
appears

in the words
of a friend

who never
spoke to you

again.
The only one

is the final
one

you see
when you are

about to leave,
and the only

one
is the only one

who breathes
with you

among
the bereaved.

The only one
is the mirror

above
and the mirror

below,
the only one

not dressed
in daylight

or starlight.
The only one

is two
and he

is you.

Blame

Blame the refrain of the backroom ballad
my boozy British grandfather

sang before dinner
as the reason

the boys in our family
never shed a public tear.

She doesn't love me now,
but it's no use to pine

rang out above the spread
of red leaf salad

and well-done beef
as sad Nana hovered

over sherry
while we puzzled

over *pine*
which was to us

a simple tree
joined with others

of its kind
to form a jail of shade

holding lost orphans,
goblins, and delirious

back-in-the-day wraiths
like granddad

singing songs
passed onto me

along with drinking
until reeling

but never weeping.

My Dog, the Past

I.

I hear him approaching
the back of my deck chair
overlooking this studio
apartment's parking lot,
not wanting to interrupt
but he'll soon crane around
and present himself in different shapes—
rueful child; friend in need;
the boss who knows best—
yet when I stand I find nothing
there of flesh and blood,
just the fading sound
of a resigned pet
returning to his bed.
So I won't be leading
him past the parish hall
and Elmhurst Lanes
to the abandoned
corner lot of tire rims
and Queen Anne's Lace,
the place where many
first-time thirsts were quenched—
sex, dope, the will to hurt,
and death when a drunk
dropped from a roof.

2.

A dog I'd seen downtown
climbs two flights
to this tiny terrace,
places a well-worn bone
at my feet and says,
"This is the horizon
you've traded for the years."
I had planned to spend
the evening on this porch
but the signifying mongrel
and his barter bone
send me to the ground floor,
having shut the begging past
behind a locked door.
Cherry blossoms wave
like hands at a parade
I used to lead,
but now I'm led,
where I used to speak,
but now I listen
to the falling petals
cutting the air,
the edge of each
a beautiful blade
and the mesmerizing horizon
drawing near.

Prayer at the Masked Ball

Be my god,
if you don't mind

being asked.
And if you don't mind

being asked
to dance

at this masked ball,
allow me

to introduce myself—
I've worn this face

since birth,
and now I want

it off.
I need a god

to remake me,
not in his image,

but in the shape
of boys

I ached to be:
the cresting

wave-like pompadour
of Johnny Villar,

Terence Kelly's
stiff upper lip,

the name alone
of Artie Robb.

If you do
become my god,

let the chandelier's
refracted constellations

strut across
each dancer's mask,

those romantic glances
of cut crystal

giving us
our best chance

of living life
as someone else.

Replace my skin
with a pelt

from smelted ore—
I'm tired

of flinching
from a score

of imagined hurts.
You always were

and always will be,
you have an infinite future

and a past as long—
so, as you glide across

this ballroom floor,
lift your disguise

and show me who you are.
I'm not asking you

to be the god
of a saint,

just of a minor sinner.
And really, who have I ever hurt?

(Yes, but *long* ago.)
Be my god

and let me recall
the good days

in our home,
not the drama of gin

before dinner
and brandy later,

where hour after hour,
the bear

went over the mountain
only to find

another mountain.
I don't need a large part

of you,
just that corner

that loves puns,
a kind of school-crossing

god,
the jester

who invented sex,
the magician

who pulls a man
out of a boy

and a new man
out of him.

My god! Good god! God forbid!
God asked to damn

everything on earth—
the lost ring, shut store,

stripped screw
and missing oar,

all who walk
on two legs,

four,
with tail or without,

employ wings,
slide on stomachs,

swim.
God asked to bless

everything we eat
and both sides

of warring nation-beasts.
God,

on whose knee
I will sit in heaven,

please be my god
before the certain curtain call.

I know
I've created you,

and I know
it's the other way around,

but since these are only
pleas on a page

don't punish me
too harshly

for being,
in a manner of speaking,

your god.
I made you

to remake me
and then

take me
to someone

who will love me,
if it's possible

to love a man
in a mask

who asks god
to dance

at the masked ball.

II

The Heart Has Reasons

And I wrote those reasons
on the ruled grid

of an index card
to preserve the moment, Madam,

when the panels of the hotel
elevator closed,

leaving just us.
A sigh and a kiss

did nicely, Lady,
but when the doors

opened again,
you were again nowhere

near, and now
the file card's lost too,

with its logical
numerical slate.

I've misplaced this and that
over the years, Dear,

but the things I miss most, Miss,
are listed on that card.

The Letters

1.

Letters written decades ago
arrive in a bundle
from a benevolent ex.

Words I put
into a young man's mouth
return to mine.

2.

Phrase by phrase, I move my lips
like someone learning to read.

Over time,
the dummy tells the ventriloquist
what to say.

3.

Pounded keys
from an IBM Selectric
have punctured a few pages.

If you lift one to the light,
a constellation appears.

4.

Each signature's etched
as if on the wall of a cell.

The author's gone—released
on time served? Escaped?

Execution is a kind of pardon,
the warden told me
when I visited Auburn Prison.

5.

I feel a thread unspool
from school to work,

romance to divorce,
from sober to blotto

to blackout and back.

6.

after Tranströmer

My house is all skylight and daylight—
panels and transoms
look through to the bay.

One pane's cloudy with a broken seal:
the watermarked page where I'll write my reply.

7.

What tone to take?
A note of thanks?
Remorse

or flirtatious
epistolary horseplay?

Asking these questions
of myself is absurd,
almost insane.

Yet decade after decade,
I've brought my life
to life
in just this way.

8.

The postmarks recall
crossing a bridge

above a dry riverbed
to buy stamps.

The span served no purpose
but continued

over that blunt gorge
as traffic

traded one side
for another,

swapped farewells
for arrivals,

destinations
for just passing through.

9.

There's still a pulse
in these return-to-sender pages.

Their wish to seduce
and secure

came true just halfway.
Blood daubs the flap

where a paper cut
sliced a lip or tongue.

She understood
some of what the writer

bled, but not everything.
Should he say it now?

Are years sufficient
to measure time?

Ask the hornet
on the arm

of the white wicker chair
this cold fall day.

His unsteady
struggling tells it all.

The Blue Sea Motel

The bench by the entrance
to the Blue Sea Motel

is where I fell for you again
after so many seasons

building castles
in the sand,

men out of snow
and raising countless

toasts at midnight
in a garden

of ice figures
carved to life

in the old year
and disappearing

hours later
in the new.

Sunrise above the neon sign
seemed a fitting

but unnecessary monstrance—
I was already praying

I wouldn't lose
my place

among the other placeholders
in your heart.

The splintered bench
seemed the only

steady thing
along that string of doors

unlocked by different hands
with the same key.

The Blue Sea faced nothing
even slightly aquatic

just waves
of warm asphalt

that shimmered
like a mirage

to those looking
at the past

and calling that split second
of hope

the future.

Love Poem (Tentative Title)

She loves the ballet and the Charleston,
the lilies of Monet and the engine

of my broken-down Venza.
When the deafening din of CNN

dominates our precinct,
she rescues me by pointing out

the art in heart, and opening up
the file in the profile I love.

Her smile can be slim
but also the merriest at the party

that spans weeks of victims
leveling charges.

She has felt that hurt herself,
but glides through

so she's both present and absent,
everywhere at once, like air.

The dance floor clears, the music rests,
and that's when the gods appear,

their great arm strength winging me
toward her, a shard skipping into the lake.

Does the lake need another stone,
or the stone so tempestuous a ride?

Reader, that's for you to decide.
Does he love her, and she, him?

Is this a love poem?
If yes, will their love survive?

Here and There

Neither here nor there,
both here and there,

our son, the one
we never had,

dictates these words
which I record,

obedient and awed
by the power

of that perfect soul
who never took a breath

but who stirred
this anonymous mist

between the two of us.
Neither here nor there,

his name won't appear
in the census,

table of contents
or any index.

First a blessing
then despair—

the hem of a christening dress,
the north star's flare

reflected
in a compass

lost somewhere
between the two of us,

neither here nor there.

Last Things First

The one who makes you
laugh is the one
who'll make you cry,

my mother used
to sigh at me,
but let's not waste time

critiquing matters
of the heart,
and instead try the door

to my often stalling car
and hope the engine starts.
Give me a push

and climb along
the running board.
The avenue is full

of danger, fear and joy.
We pass a boy
swinging a basket

toward the sky,
headed toward
a cliff he might not see.

Why should he?
Whether he finds
a ledge or a cloud,

he's free.
We've missed
the overture, the aria,

but the encore's all
we need—
no more fiddling

for the condo key
or anxious heading
toward the bedroom door—

we'll just wake up
at dawn.
We've paid our dues

on time, stood in line
and signed our names.
We've put first things first,

and been in accord
with the sumptuary laws.
Now let's reject

the order of the day,
throw it in reverse
from Z to A.

Give me a shove
and leap after me.

Annie Came for the Apples

"Annie came for the apples. I died all day."
Someone wrote a poem that began
that way. I can't recall his name,
but I've never forgotten Annie
who came for the apples and left with a life.
I wonder if that poet first wrote *cried*.
They go together, hand in hand,
and take turns preceding
and following each other.
Annie remains missing, as invisible
as the hyperbolic poet, although
she has a name, and a soul too,
if you swing that way.
She must be dead herself by now,
maybe never knowing a poet died
of love for her, and passed his passion
to another in the anonymous
brotherhood of the brokenhearted
who wrote a poem that began,
"Annie came for the apples. I died all day."

That's the Hell We're In

I'm writing from down here
among the overheated meek

who didn't inherit the earth,
and the singed goblins

and boiling trolls
of unfulfilled promise.

By the way, did you tell
Adele about us?

Did you mention
that when I opened

a thriller
in that bookstore

without AC last August
the arsonist-firefighter protagonist

had your last name?
When I was a kid,

our car often died
leaving Rockaway Beach

on eighty degree days
causing my father to yell,

That's the hell we're in.
Some say there's a way out,

that God forgives,
but I haven't survived

his last judgment.
I lost him

between the flame
and the cinder,

the boardwalk
and the splinter.

I lost him
in my devotion

to that unholy trinity
of me, myself and I.

Speaking of identity,
I'm wondering

if you signed your last letter
Love,

or were those spikey marks
the legs of a crushed bug?

That's the hell we're in.
We believed

a Broadway play
would bring a dose of cheer

but the drama began
before the curtain rose:

a man clubbed his son
on the shoulder

with a rolled-up program,
and the rotund buffo

beside me
emptied a bag

of licorice vines
onto his warm lap

and I could hear him
eating the nearly silent

surreptitious treat
until the curtain fell.

That's the hell we're in.

Alphabet

I love you is such an inadequate way of saying *I love you.*
—Joan Crawford in *Possessed*

Everything falls short
even a skirt
trying to hold its own
against the wind
so I will bet
on Mother Nature
every time
I see a gust
make its way
across the street
to the bus stop
where you wait
as if for me
though I know
you are really
going to work
but I can have
the wind blow where
and when I want
all the while aware
it is only art,
an alphabet,
a few marks on a page
not nearly
what I meant to say.

Last Act

Your blouse on the stair,
a powder smudge

at the edge of the tub,
the mirror asking

your face
to bring it to life

the way
color creates light.

And by the chair,
a half-done script

describing
the bare bones set

I'm keeping intact
along with assuring

the one actor
who hasn't left

he won't be alone.

Invisible Eden

I met you in autumn
inside an autumn apple

neglected on the orchard floor.
Friends leaning ladders

called for us to join them
but we stayed in that sphere

I hoped would never
disappear despite

each changing season.
The ink on this page

will fade if I mention
Eden—

poems are better suited
to invoking the inferno

though there's something
to be said for a naked couple

in a garden bed
where a snake holds court.

You stayed with me,
a kind of *nature morte*,

but as the noir writer noted:
no matter the circumstance,

setting, or high feelings at stake,
there is just one theme—

things are not what they seem.

Home

Her car turned left,
you watched it go,
the revving engine
ransacked the songs
of chickadees and wrens
among the branches
of the shrubs
her fender brushed,
leaving just a place to park.
No sign of smoke
from the exhaust,
no trace of the spark
that started her off,
not even an echo
of the final door.
How far will she go,
how near would you get
if you were to follow?
These questions abolish time
as you stand
in that vacated rectangle
visible from the street,
in the center
of the missing length
of crimson steel
that meant her name,
her face, her hands
upon the wheel that turned
the world around.
She's across the bridge by now.

Anniversary

I hear the rain
more clearly,
see my throat

in the morning mirror
not merely as
a funnel-neck

for booze.
Lost the weight
I tried to lose.

Friends came and went.
I learned to sit
like a block

of cement
while servers pranced
with trays

holding tumblers
of truth
and loud mouth soup,

asking which, for whom.
There's still an itch
as I introduce myself

to a new face
reflected in the glass,
invite that well-adjusted

trespasser of a man
to dance
and am refused.

The Great Deviled Eggs of the World

The first thing I recall is a falling tray
of deviled eggs
when I opened the refrigerator door,
splashing my shirt, shorts
and legs before it hit the floor,
leaving my mother
and her bridge club just the dregs.
The uproar was so great
I can still see the runny mess
that even the most imaginative hen
could not anticipate.
And the eggs, no longer
oval with loneliness,
embraced the boy about to taste
the condiments of fate.

My Mother, Heidegger and Derrida

Educated at a school in Queens
whose slim roster of celebrated alums

boasts Don Rickles number one,
my mother knew little about art,

but she took me to a show
where she withdrew into private air

on seeing *The Potato Eaters*
and *Three Pairs of Shoes*

because the shoes resembled my grandmother's
high-topped boots my mother knelt before

and laced up every morning
after applying salve

to those diabetes-ulcerated shins.
And the potatoes recalled the fires

she and her brothers built
against the curb:

charred skin, raw at the center,
and called *mickeys* in honor of the Irish.

My mother pointed out how the poor
have only potatoes for dinner, their faces

so rough they looked unearthed themselves.
And the shoes, ravaged by labor. Unlike Heidegger,

who said of *Three Pairs of Shoes*—
"From the dark opening of the worn insides

the toilsome tread of the worker stares forth,"
and utterly unlike Derrida, whose note on that painting

questioned what "constitutes a pair of shoes and how
the elements of such combine different forms of reality,"

my mother said they show how hard some people work.

Oncle Lily

Oncle Lily from overseas
inhales with an activist's vigilance

the perfume from his nephew's
garden on Cape Cod,

a dedicated countdown:
1-2-3—Breathe out!

Roses lose their composure
in the storm—

it's as if he stowed
the Gauloises and Gitanes smog

above Champs-Élysées cafes
and now expels it hard toward

the honey-skinned, parasol-twirling
beach nymphs who spatter

us with dreams of not wilting
at their hems. Did I forget to say

they danced a ring around him?
They did, and he dissolved quickly,

not in smoke, but in thought.

His Shirt

The striped shirt drying
on the patio chair—
you can say he wore
that shirt,
its back covered
his back,
framed him
against the car seat
when we drove
to Jones Beach.
Upright as he walked,
horizontal
where he tossed it
to the sand,
damp when he
dressed again.
You can say you bought
that shirt, it fit,
it looked okay on the boy
who gave it life
before life
left it here on the chair.

The Second Olga

My grandmother had eight children,
one of them twice.

The first Olga lived
a mere month,

succeeded by my mother,
the second Olga,

dragged from childhood
each Sunday

to face her fate—
a stone

at Calvary Cemetery
carved with her name.

She treated the maze of graves
as a game, a way

of dealing with the world
that ended

only when she rested
next to her sister.

A lifetime of wishing
the rules clear:

winners and losers apart,
the dead and the living

unmistakably divided
into horizontal

versus vertical shapes.
And gender—

a simple matter
of pink or blue

unlike the tangled impulses
that sparked

her fiery nature as a girl
when she spun

a vicious
cat's eye marble

off her thumb,
and held her own

in a knife-flinging game
of five-finger fillet.

Street play gave way
to checkers, chess,

crosswords and acrostics,
extending later

to her irrepressible accounting
as a householder

of each spent cent:
TV tubes, sauterne,

sugar cubes and soap.
Her diary a ledger

of lifeless figures,
no narrative,

no spilled memories,
everything measured,

everything contained,
and in the back

of the book,
a floridly engraved

Irish Sweepstakes receipt,
offering reincarnation,

a change of luck,
and the hope against hope

against hope
of being born again.

The Death of Zero

"After Virtue" by Wim Mertens played at the two-injection death
of Zero, a bulldog mix and runt of an early litter, but the soul of my
stolid friend hasn't healed. Her shovel-face still knocks against rungs
and table legs, scraping the shag rug for crumbs. The vet called her
dim when I brought her in to fix a crumpled hip from leaping off
our upper deck, and again when joining boozy swimmers scaling the
seawall. Estranged from time and space, she looked alert at just one
place: passing a chain-link fence neatly vandalized by wire cutters for
kids to crawl through. She stared as if considering this a smart way
to escape. From what? The laws of house and yard and leash? Her face
and fate? I think of her on stormy days when I had to drag her from
the garden where she sat immobile in the rain. She comes home on
her own when Mertens' music plays.

Unwritten

What she wanted, she never found,
my solitary aunt
who spent her retired life
at *The Edge of Night*,
before *The Secret Storm*.
No suitor carried her
across the threshold
to the role she claimed
to court: efficient,
loved and loving wife.
My smart, unmarried aunt
was proud of having
nothing to hide
and would show
to any curious mind
the pressed and cheerful
bounty of her hope chest.
My youth coincided
with her prime
and she matched me
to a summer job
at the eastside office
where she shuffled files.
From home to work,
we rode the subway
back and forth,
AM and PM—bookends
bracing an unread book.
In the final days of August
I crossed the line she drew
through her calendar,
the highway the tour bus took
that brought us to D.C.
A room for two,
a three-day stay

unlike our commute's
parallel tracks
but a similar route to the story
in that book,
open but still unread,
unread because unwritten,
even now.

Last Words, Last Rites, Last Acts

One wondered where he parked his car.
A mother asked, "Why'd you write that book?"

The priest said it was a bridge
too far to think paradise was in the cards

for a soul away from church so long.
One kept crying, "Dry my tears."

Another bowed to kiss a cross
and left some spit upon the Lord.

My aunt got angry when a niece
fit a cell phone to her ear

and sighed, "Say goodbye to Cousin Faye."
The pest kept crying, "Dry my tears."

My father complained his place in line
had disappeared just as he was near

to paying the cashier for a triple berry pie.
My grandmother said she had something

in her eye.
My roofer grandfather didn't have time

to tell what was on his mind
because the scaffold fell.

A poet said, "Don't ask about the tolling bell."
The refrain we grew sick of hearing

was the sissy crying, "Dry my tears."
Another, standing bedside

and staring at the ceiling,
said he saw a god

who didn't care about sparrows,
hunger, war and strife,

or plans to gain eternal life.
He transcribed that writing on the wall

by scrawling across a pad
his memories of relatives and friends,

his mom and dad,
whose funerals left him

in arrears, and he signed off
with a line better written one less time,

"Dry my tears."

Oldies Night at the Riverbottom

A man in the corner with the imprint
of a vaccine on his shoulder

snares the eye of a girl
chewing nicotine

who is sipping something
someone sent over.

His drink's replaced by a drink
with fresh power

while on bar stools
figures devour figurines

and vice versa
to the tune of "Crimson and Clover."

Calvary Cemetery

I'm here with my mother
rubbing moss off a stone:
the dates are clear,
the parenthesis closed.
Three notes from a warbler
high in the pines
compete with a couple
sparring over grooming a plot.
One shakes a trowel
at the other's
festooned pot of mums.
Above the avenue,
the neon letters *tv*
flash in the Stevens
Appliance sign
alongside Bulova Watch
and My-T-Fine.
All around us,
the dead hope to rise
and the living bring
their grief to light.

It

It was there the day
you opened your eyes.

It ran in the veins
of both pairs of hands

that guided you
through childhood.

Was it bright, was it dark,
did you look away

from the start, or dare
a path toward it?

Were you really that dumb
or was it really that smart?

It brought wit to your tongue
and gave you the nerve

to ask an angel to hold you.
You were here, you were there,

raising cheer north and south:
Bottoms Up! Down the Hatch!

accompanied by a sax and kazoo.
They say it's a gift,

and it's a gift
to think so, but if it came

from a friend,
you'd never see him again.

Cabin

The kerosene lantern lights the single room
twice as brightly
when placed before a mirror.

I'm reading the same book
as the shadow along the armrest
but where I see a simple story,

it claims an opaque plot,
where I feel a jolt of hope,
it gives an ironic smile,

and when I check
how far I've gotten,
it counts just those pages left.

Like the lamp and its reflection,
we merge
only when the flame goes out.

Lifespan of the Average Man

I'm waiting for a sign
that says my pulse
is strong,

my reflexes fair
despite the years,
and that making

the long trip
to meet her
is not entirely wrong.

Time will tell.
Time will also kill
those who call life

a living.
Life doesn't call itself that,
life waits for you

to name it,
and regret claims it
if you stall.

The sign finally came
when the minute hand
fell from the face

of the clock on the wall,
freed from the task
of keeping time

but not stopping it.
The remaining hand
stuttered in place,

and then,
having the stage
to itself,

spoke, saying,
"It's too late
to ask the past

how it feels.
It lies at the base
of the dial,

a spade beside a grave.
Now I live
in the so-called moment,

a finite part
of an infinite plan.
Do you call

this stopped heart
a model
of how to live

and what to do?
There is no difference
between day and night

from my point of view."

Ex

There's no more we, no more
you and I alive in a parenthesis

we called home, no more
flinches, clinches, pulled punches,

winces, no more horizon
almost in reach, no breaking

through the ribbon at the finish line,
no ballyhoo against the backdrop

of sailboats, breezes, canoes
and water skiers

at the cottage
with the shore for a front door,

no more calling, seeking,
saluting, cheering

the burning vista visible
from the dock, the deck,

the flying bridge,
there's just a struck clock,

a stained ring around
the inside of the empty

coffee cup that last touched your lips.

Erase Nothing

The secondhand rustic
wrought iron standing lamp

looks over my shoulder
as I turn page after page

of handwritten letters,
each sheet

slight as a glance,
but stacked together

they stare hard
from under a bulb

illuminating the cursive
landscape of crosses,

anchors, loops and lines.
I tilt the shade

to coax more light
and cannot hide

my shame that these
are letters I wrote

to you and never mailed,
each sentence

fierce, romantic, lost
in clouds

through which
there rose the mountains

of if, maybe and suppose.

Signs from Above

A doe picks you out
of the helpless crowd
at the crosswalk

and nears
your nervous sleeve
before getting spooked

and slain
by a pickup truck
off Main Street.

On the walk home,
down a lane by the lake,
two blackbirds

land in your way
and do not flinch:
emissaries

from a nearby nest,
the Lord's
kitchen cabinet,

or a Disney matinee.
They seem to know
what's best for them,

unlike the doe
caught in the cacophony
of careening metal

and exhaust.
A blown leaf
falls at your feet—

a ticket
from this impasse—
and the birds taking flight

make you think
you can live
in that standoff

where the past and future
cross swords—
a glinting moment

called the wishful present,
where the doe
retreats to the wood,

and your lost friends,
Over-tipping Tom,
I-dare-you-Claire,

and Dawn
with her famous fear
of feathers,

climb out of their corpses
and sneak down
your childhood street

one tree at a time,
closer and closer
and pine by pine.

A flock overhead
flies through the dark.
Above the carcass

of the deer,
you see the streetlights
and the stars.

The Double

I kept nothing from him,
or so I thought,

until I found the notebook
where he wrote

he preferred "Hey Joe"
to "The Cantos."

The next time
he came into my life

I was shaving
and he answered

a text from a woman
who knew he was alone

with the radio on so low
it barely trembled sound.

They agreed to meet
at a cafe overlooking

a harbor where tourists
play hide-and-seek

with the tide.
The mirror reflected him

as he had been,
and I took his place

in the glass.
He entered my car

and smoothed his hair
in the rear view—

a son, the father of a son,
and a figment

of a devastated isolato.
He was many men in one.

I'd kept nothing from him,
but what he kept from me

was the person I wanted to be.

Kitten Cat Kitten

Cat follows kitten,
sermon follows sin,

stem follows seed,
fear follows famine.

Calm follows climax,
rattle follows death,

plateau follows peak,
witness, theft.

Calf follows cattle,
fallen bridge, rust,

acrobat above the crowd,
a fatal gust of wind.

Beg follows bankrupt,
chicken, an egg,

used to follows *can,*
I'm not, I am.

Pause follows pulse,
and god bless,

goddamn.
Goodbye follows greeting,

high follows rush,
stiff follows supple,

breach, trust.
No one follows someone,

wind follows hat,
egg, chicken.

Kitten, a cat.

2003
Trouble, Mary Baine Campbell
A Place Made of Starlight, Peter Cooley
Taking Down the Angel, Jeff Friedman
Lives of Water, John Hoppenthaler
Imitation of Life, Allison Joseph
Except for One Obscene Brushstroke, Dzvinia Orlowsky
The Mastery Impulse, Ricardo Pau-Llosa
Casino of the Sun, Jerry Williams

2004
The Women Who Loved Elvis All Their Lives, Fleda Brown
The Chronic Liar Buys a Canary, Elizabeth Edwards
Freeways and Aqueducts, James Harms
Prague Winter, Richard Katrovas
Trains in Winter, Jay Meek
Tristimania, Mary Ruefle
Venus Examines Her Breast, Maureen Seaton
Various Orbits, Thom Ward

2005
Things I Can't Tell You, Michael Dennis Browne
Bent to the Earth, Blas Manuel De Luna
Blindsight, Carol Hamilton
Fallen from a Chariot, Kevin Prufer
Needlegrass, Dennis Sampson
Laws of My Nature, Margot Schilpp
Sleeping Woman, Herbert Scott
Renovation, Jeffrey Thomson

2006
Burn the Field, Amy Beeder
The Sadness of Others, Hayan Charara
A Grammar to Waking, Nancy Eimers
Dog Star Delicatessen: New and Selected Poems 1979–2006, Mekeel McBride
Shinemaster, Michael McFee
Eastern Mountain Time, Joyce Peseroff
Dragging the Lake, Robert Thomas

2007
Trick Pear, Suzanne Cleary
So I Will Till the Ground, Gregory Djanikian
Black Threads, Jeff Friedman
Drift and Pulse, Kathleen Halme
The Playhouse Near Dark, Elizabeth Holmes
On the Vanishing of Large Creatures, Susan Hutton
One Season Behind, Sarah Rosenblatt
Indeed I Was Pleased with the World, Mary Ruefle
The Situation, John Skoyles

2008
The Grace of Necessity, Samuel Green
After West, James Harms
Anticipate the Coming Reservoir, John Hoppenthaler
Convertible Night, Flurry of Stones, Dzvinia Orlowsky
Parable Hunter, Ricardo Pau-Llosa
The Book of Sleep, Eleanor Stanford

2009
Divine Margins, Peter Cooley
Cultural Studies, Kevin A. González
Dear Apocalypse, K. A. Hays
Warhol-o-rama, Peter Oresick
Cave of the Yellow Volkswagen, Maureen Seaton
Group Portrait from Hell, David Schloss
Birdwatching in Wartime, Jeffrey Thomson

2010
The Diminishing House, Nicky Beer
A World Remembered, T. Alan Broughton
Say Sand, Daniel Coudriet
Knock Knock, Heather Hartley
In the Land We Imagined Ourselves, Jonathan Johnson
Selected Early Poems: 1958-1983, Greg Kuzma
The Other Life: Selected Poems, Herbert Scott
Admission, Jerry Williams

2011
Having a Little Talk with Capital P Poetry, Jim Daniels
Oz, Nancy Eimers
Working in Flour, Jeff Friedman
Scorpio Rising: Selected Poems, Richard Katrovas
The Politics, Benjamin Paloff
Copperhead, Rachel Richardson

2012
Now Make an Altar, Amy Beeder
Still Some Cake, James Cummins
Comet Scar, James Harms
Early Creatures, Native Gods, K. A. Hays
That Was Oasis, Michael McFee
Blue Rust, Joseph Millar
Spitshine, Anne Marie Rooney
Civil Twilight, Margot Schilpp

2013
Oregon, Henry Carlile
Selvage, Donna Johnson
At the Autopsy of Vaslav Nijinksy, Bridget Lowe
Silvertone, Dzvinia Orlowsky
Fibonacci Batman: New & Selected Poems (1991–2011), Maureen Seaton
When We Were Cherished, Eve Shelnutt
The Fortunate Era, Arthur Smith
Birds of the Air, David Yezzi

2014
Night Bus to the Afterlife, Peter Cooley
Alexandria, Jasmine Bailey
Dear Gravity, Gregory Djanikian
Pretenders, Jeff Friedman
How I Went Red, Maggie Glover
All That Might Be Done, Samuel Green
Man, Ricardo Pau-Llosa
The Wingless, Cecilia Llompart

2015
The Octopus Game, Nicky Beer
The Voices, Michael Dennis Browne
Domestic Garden, John Hoppenthaler
We Mammals in Hospitable Times, Jynne Dilling Martin
And His Orchestra, Benjamin Paloff
Know Thyself, Joyce Peseroff
cadabra, Dan Rosenberg
The Long Haul, Vern Rutsala
Bartram's Garden, Eleanor Stanford

2016
Something Sinister, Hayan Charara
The Spokes of Venus, Rebecca Morgan Frank
Adult Swim, Heather Hartley
Swastika into Lotus, Richard Katrovas
The Nomenclature of Small Things, Lynn Pedersen
Hundred-Year Wave, Rachel Richardson
Where Are We in This Story, Sarah Rosenblatt
Inside Job, John Skoyles
Suddenly It's Evening: Selected Poems, John Skoyles

2017
Disappeared, Jasmine V. Bailey
Custody of the Eyes, Kimberly Burwick
Dream of the Gone-From City, Barbara Edelman
Sometimes We're All Living in a Foreign Country, Rebecca Morgan Frank
Rowing with Wings, James Harms
Windthrow, K. A. Hays
We Were Once Here, Michael McFee
Kingdom, Joseph Millar
The Histories, Jason Whitmarsh

2018
World Without Finishing, Peter Cooley
May Is an Island, Jonathan Johnson
The End of Spectacle, Virginia Konchan

Big Windows, Lauren Moseley
Bad Harvest, Dzvinia Orlowsky
The Turning, Ricardo Pau-Llosa
Immortal Village, Kathryn Rhett
No Beautiful, Anne Marie Rooney
Last City, Brian Sneeden
Imaginal Marriage, Eleanor Stanford
Black Sea, David Yezzi

2019
Brightword, Kimberly Burwick
The Complaints, W. S. Di Piero
Ordinary Chaos, Kimberly Kruge
Blue Flame, Emily Pettit
Afterswarm, Margot Schilpp

2020
Build Me a Boat, Michael Dennis Browne
Sojourners of the In-Between, Gregory Djanikian
The Marksman, Jeff Friedman
Disturbing the Light, Samuel Green
Any God Will Do, Virginia Konchan
My Second Work, Bridget Lowe
Flourish, Dora Malech
Petition, Joyce Peseroff
Take Nothing, Deborah Pope

2021
The One Certain Thing, Peter Cooley
The Knives We Need, Nava EtShalom
Oh You Robot Saints!, Rebecca Morgan Frank
Dark Harvest: New & Selected Poems, 2001–2020, Joseph Millar
Glorious Veils of Diane, Rainie Oet
Yes and No, John Skoyles